The History of Torture

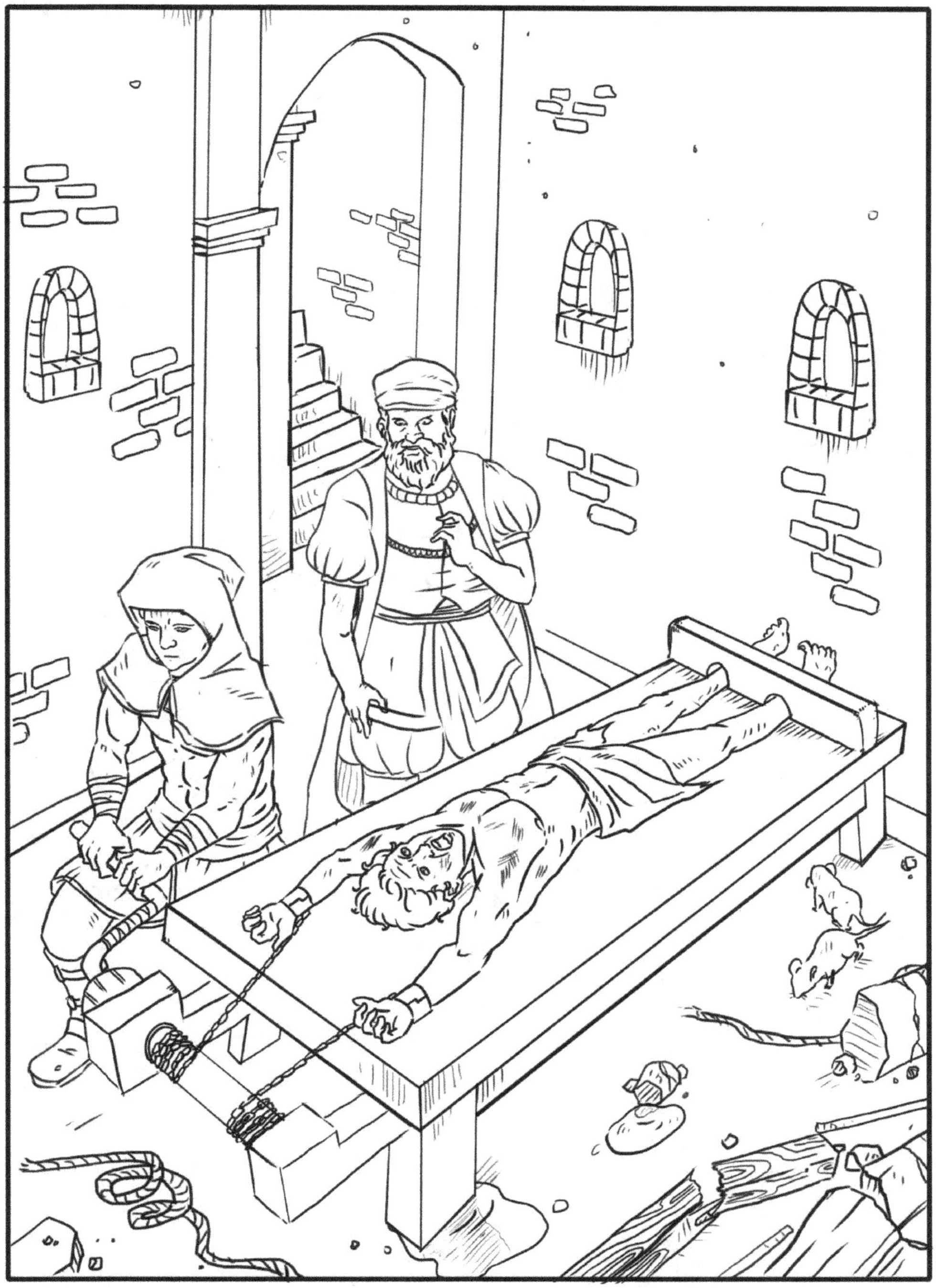

Adult Coloring Book
By Giovanni Verbania

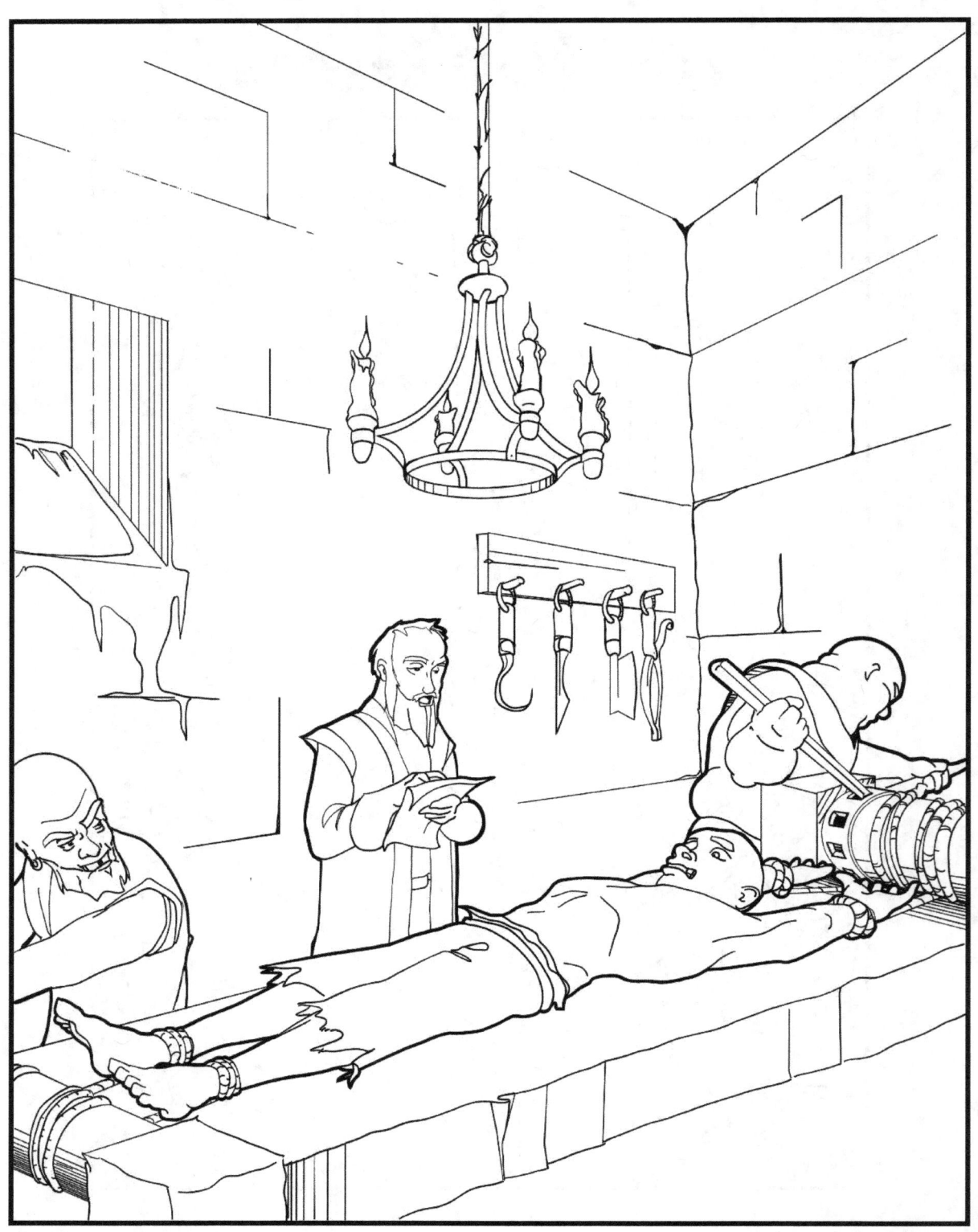

Note from the Author

18 Horrible images lie ahead… for this coloring book about torture is intended not only as a relaxing activity to soothe the nerves after a hard day, but also as a lesson in human history, cruelty, intolerance, and stupidity. The book contains graphic scenes of violence and is not intended for children that you don't want to scare and traumatize into doing their goddamned chores for once.

Painstaking research when into each image. Illustrators slaved over each scene to provide historical accuracy and period details. We really held their feet to the fire!

Think carefully: who is your worst enemy? Who owes you money? Remember your mom or older brother? When is the last time your boss gave you a raise? Can you picture them in each scene? Of course you can!

So kick back, get out your pens and pencils, and let your imagination run wild as you color your way back through the ages…especially the Dark Ages! You're bound to love it!

Giovanni Verbania

Edited by Jennifer Anne Gomez

**Copyright © 2017 Verbania
All Rights Reserved**

**ISBN-13:978-1979807517
ISBN-10: 1979807515**

COLOR TEST PAGE

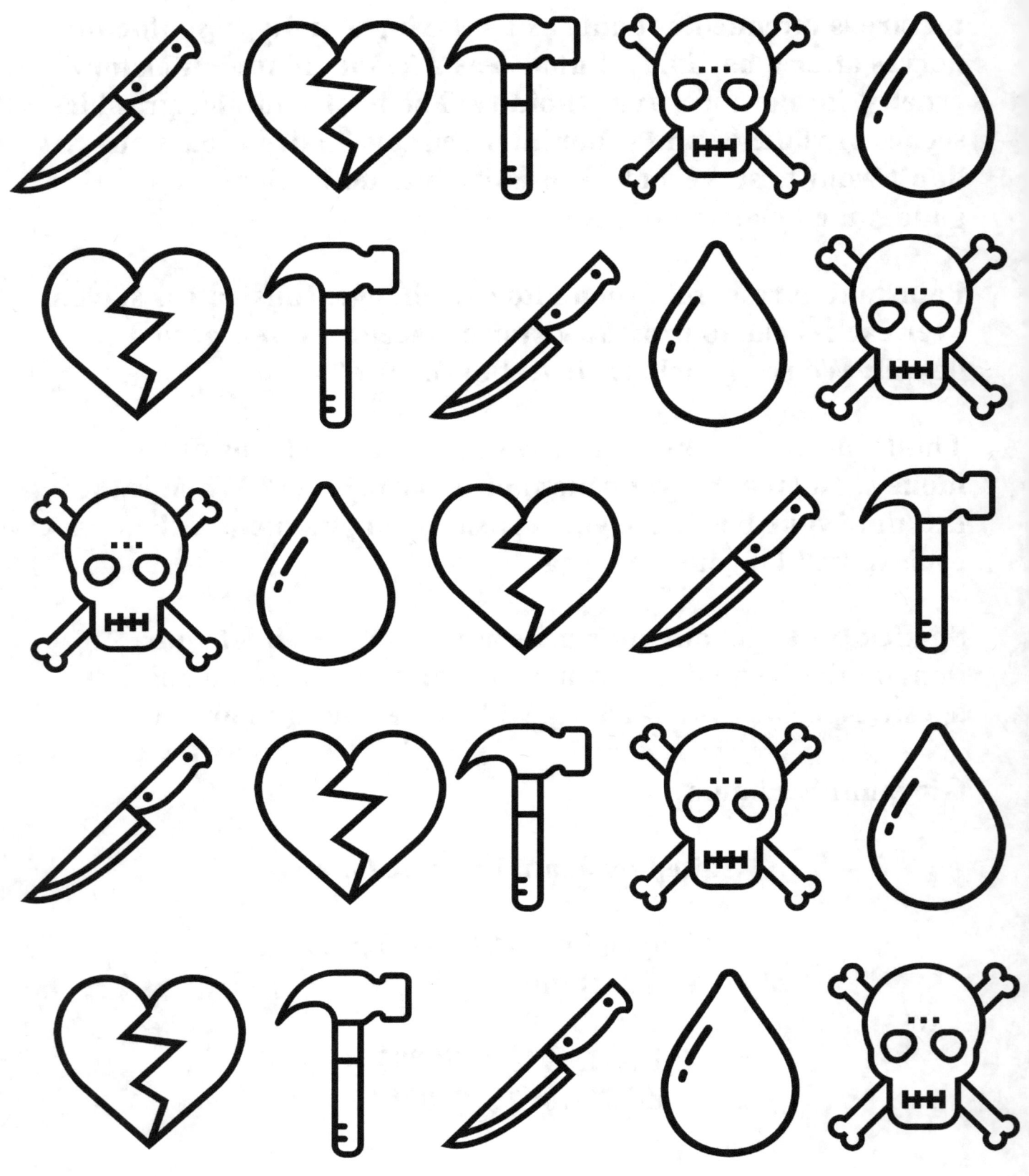

Contents

The Rack
Keelhauling
Iron Maiden
Thumbscrews
Dunking
Mask of Shame
Chair of Torture
Wooden Horse
The Pillory
Flogging
Spanish Tickler
Strappado
Waterboarding
Foot roasting
Heretic's Fork
Shrew's Fiddle
Water Cure
Drunkard's Cloak

The Rack

The rack was an extremely painful form of torture wherein the victim was slowly stretched apart. Their arms and feet were tied to large spools and a torturer turned a handle which slowly tightened the ropes. Typically used until a confession was made, bones were broken and limbs torn off if the interrogation went on too long.

The rack was an ancient torture device. Alexander the Great had his court historian, Callisthenes, tortured on the rack when his plot to murder the young conqueror was uncovered.

In AD 65, Gaius Calpurnius Piso, a leading Roman statesman, formed a plot to assassinate the despotic emperor Nero in what came to be known as the Pisonian conspiracy. A woman named Epicharis who knew of the plot was caught and tortured on the rack until she revealed the names of the conspirators. On the way to a second session, she strangled herself.

In 304 AD, Saint Vincent of Saragossa, was tortured on the rack as part of Roman Emperor Diocletian's persecution of Christianity in Spain. He died shortly after in prison, a Catholic martyr.

In 1307, King Philip "The Fair" of France, deeply in debt to the Knights Templar, sought to destroy their order and steal their treasure. With the help of his puppet, Pope Clement V, the Knights were rounded up and tortured by the hundreds. Many gave false confessions or died on the rack.

Spanish inquisitors made extensive use of the rack during the Spanish Inquisition of 1478 AD-1808 AD. Napoleon abolished the practice after his invasion of Spain.

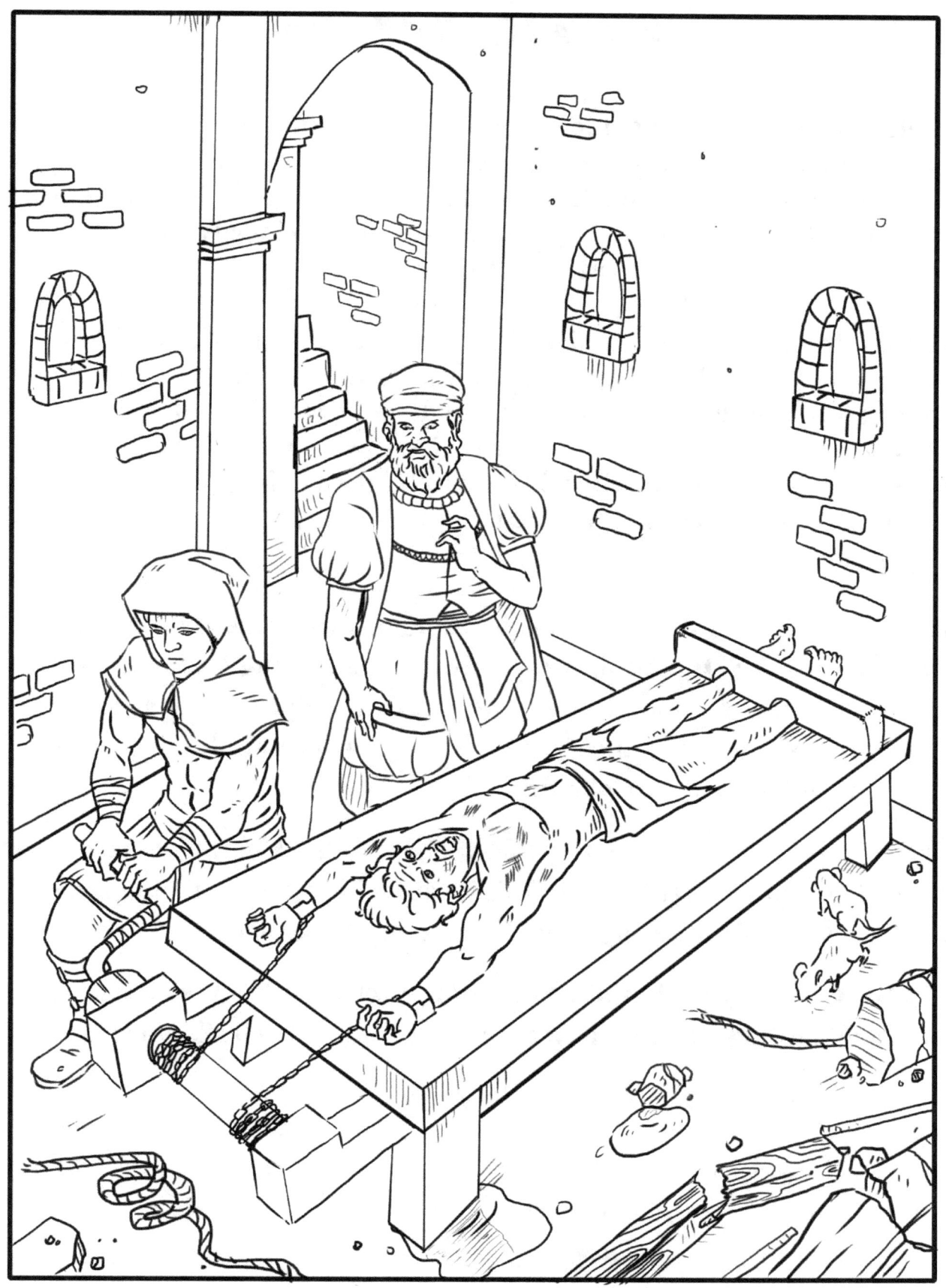

Keelhauling

Keelhauling was a punishment and torture method used by sailors dating back to Ancient Greece. This method was first mentioned as a punishment for piracy in the Rhodian Maritime Code (Lex Rhodia), from 800 BC. An image of an unlucky Greek mariner is pictured being keelhauled on a vase from the same era.

The sailor would be stripped and tied so he couldn't swim and have weights tied to his legs. He was then attached to a rope that ran underneath the ship, thrown overboard, and dragged under the ship against the razor sharp barnacles. Pulled back on deck, the process could be repeated as the captain saw fit. If the victim was dragged too fast, they could be ripped to shreds or even decapitated. Too slow, and they would drown.

The British Navy introduced keelhauling as punishment in the 11th century with the Dutch following suit in 1560, calling it Kielhalen. While many fictional accounts exist of pirates administering justice through "walking the plank," the truth is that keelhauling was their preferred method of punishment.

Keelhauling was sensationalized in the 1935 film *Mutiny on the Bounty* where the brutality of Captain Bligh was evidenced by his flogging a dead man and keelhauling. Neither actually took place.

The Dutch finally outlawed this brutal practice in 1853. Today, the term keelhauling survives as a term meaning, "to rebuke severely."

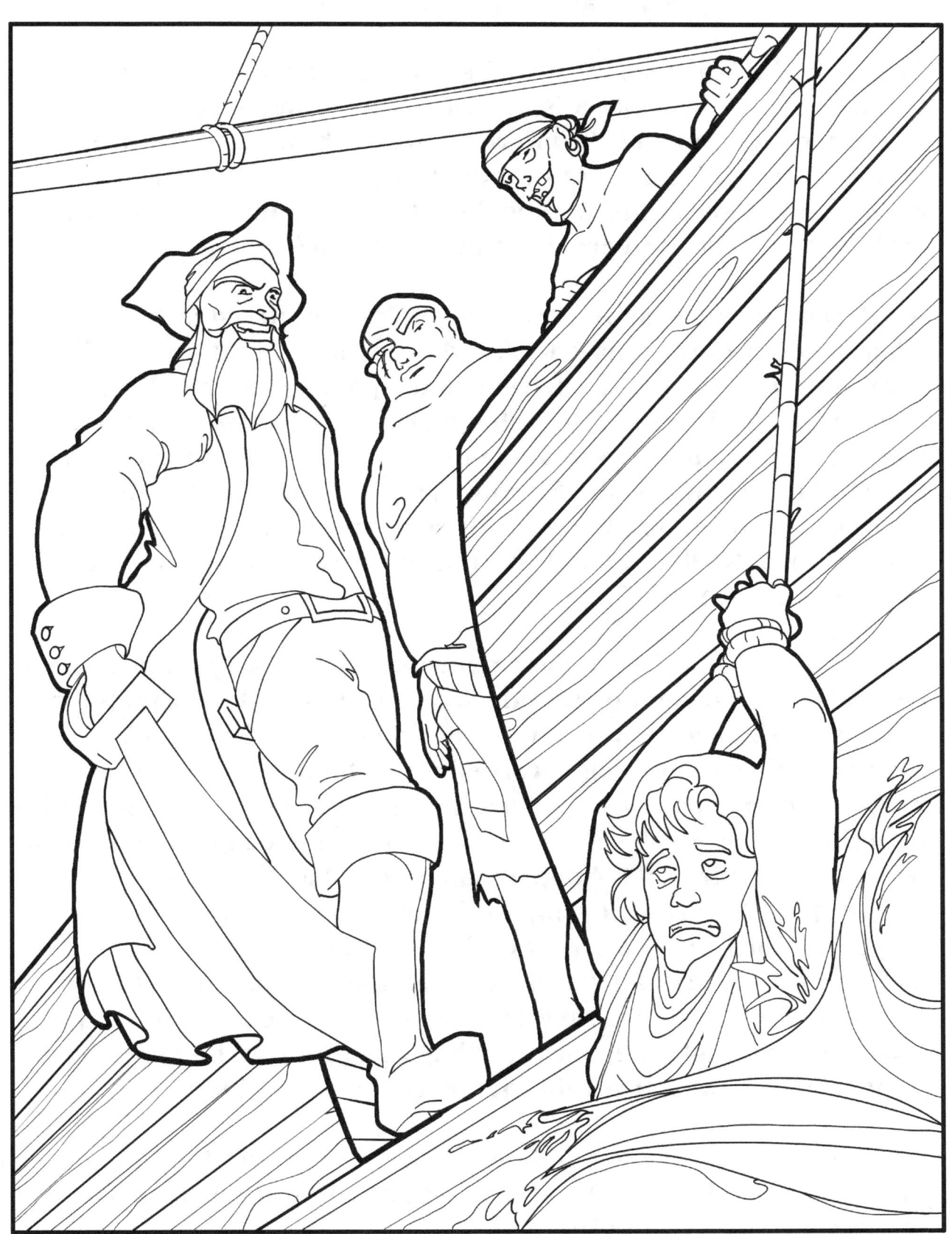

Iron Maiden

The Iron Maiden is the most well-known and frequently depicted torture device. Typically it is depicted as a coffin-shaped wood box, with a female head, and an interior lined with spikes. Victims were placed inside and the doors shut to impale them. Appearing in countless cartoons, films and books, the Iron Maiden symbolizes medieval brutality and cruelty. But was it real?

A reference to an execution with the maiden occurred in 1515, wherein a forger of coins was placed inside an Iron Maiden. "The doors shut slowly, so that the very sharp points penetrated his arms and legs, his belly, chest, eyes, shoulders, and his buttocks, but not enough to kill him." He screamed for two days, after which he died. Known in Germany as the Eiserne Jungfrau, the most famous example was the Iron Maiden of Nuremberg, first displayed as far back as 1802. Sadly, this torture treasure was destroyed in allied bombings during WW2.

Many historians think maidens were recreated from misunderstood translations of ancient torture device descriptions. Inspiration for these devilish devices may have come from the ancient execution of Marcus Atilius Regulus as recorded in Tertullian's *To the Martyrs* in which the Carthaginians "packed him into a tight wooden box, spiked with sharp nails on all sides so that he could not lean in any direction without being pierced." Another source for the idea could have been the Apega of Nabis. According to the ancient Greek historian Polybius, King Nabis, a tyrant of Sparta, had a device made in the image of his greedy and merciless wife, Apega. The device's arms, hands, and breasts were covered with nails. Those who did not pay their taxes willingly, were sent to "hug the queen." This triggered the arms to enclose and crush the victim until they paid up!

The psychopathic son of Saddam Hussein, Uday, was found to have an iron maiden at the Iraqi Football Association headquarters. The spikes were worn from use.

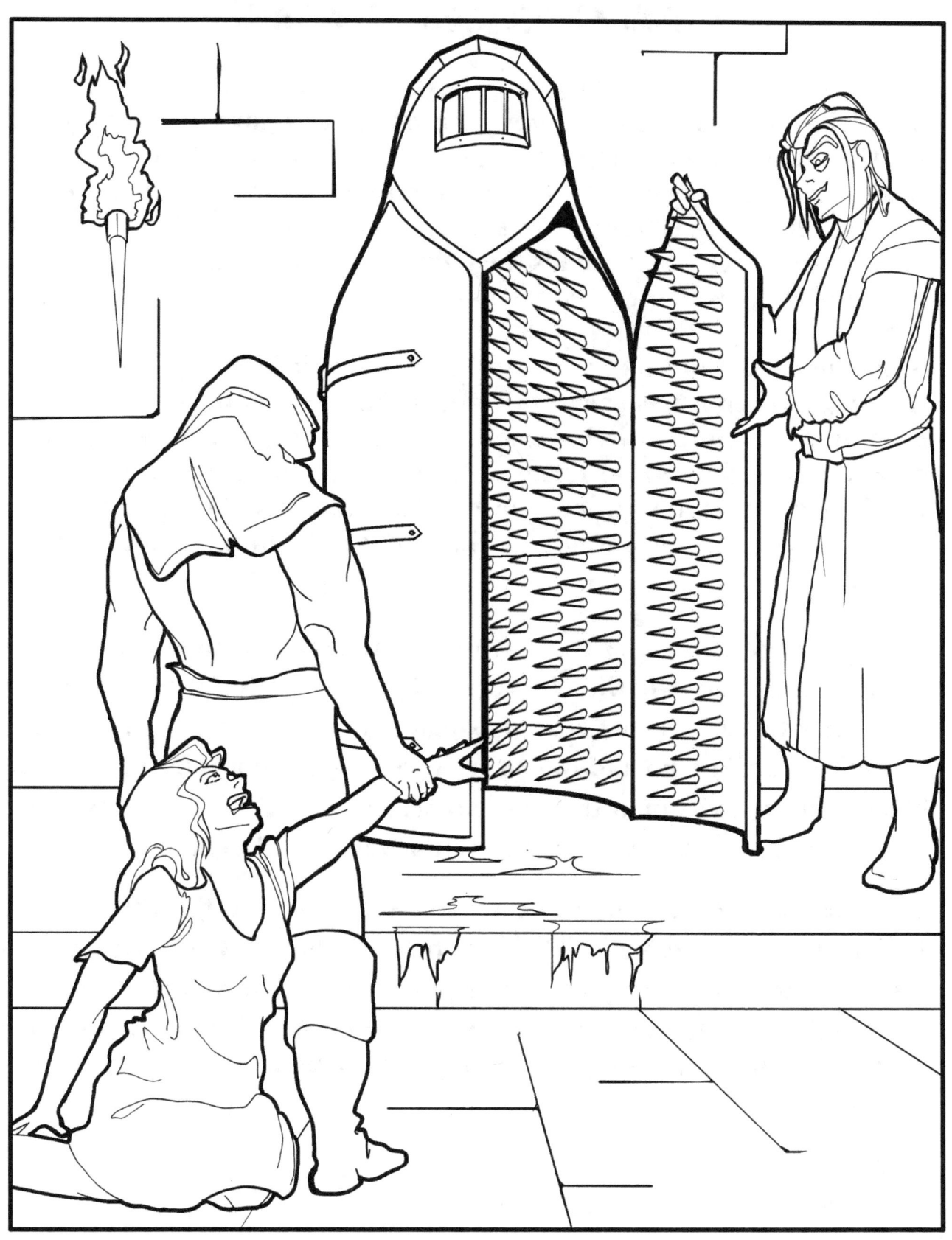

Thumbscrews

Small and portable, thumbscrews were the ideal pain-delivery system for the medieval torturer on the go. This simple but effective device was used to slowly crush fingers or toes in an iron vice. Often these were applied with so much force as to swell the arms of the sufferer up to their shoulders. Sometimes the bars upon which the digits lay contained spikes to increase the pain.

Also known as thumbkins, thumbikens, pillywinks and pilnie-winks, the first written reference to this finger fracturer appeared in an account of supposed witch Aleson Balfour and her role in a plot to assassinate of the Earl of Orkney. Her seven-year-old daughter had her fingers crushed until her mother "confessed" to being a witch. She retracted her confession, but was later strangled and burned at the stake.

A more famous case was that involving the female Italian Baroque painter Artemisia Gentileschi. Raped by her painting tutor, Agostino Tassi, her father pressed charged against him. In a cruel twist of fate, it was Artemisia who had to endure torture by thumbscrews to prove she had been a virgin at the time she was raped. Tassi was convicted and sentenced to a year in prison but never served a day.

Thumbscrews were also used extensively on slaves in the 18th and 19th centuries. Notable British abolitionist Thomas Clarkson carried a set with him to elicit sympathy for the enslaved and as part of his call to eliminate the vile practice. Slavery was finally outlawed in most of the British Empire with the passage of the Slavery Abolition Act of 1833.

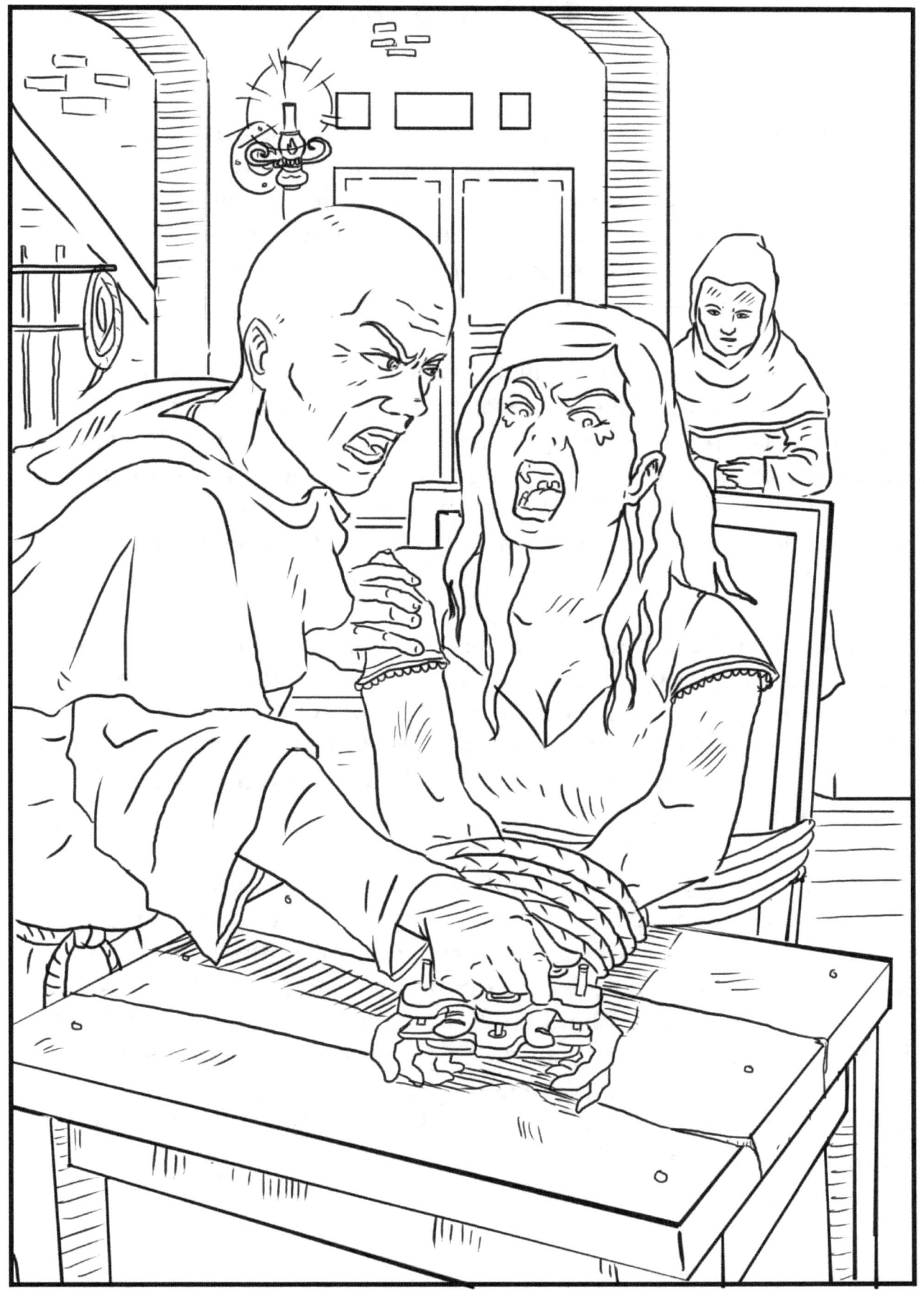

Dunking

Dunking was an ancient form of judicial practice known as Trial by Ordeal in which guilt or innocence was determined by a dangerous experience such as combat, fire, or in this case - water. A long plank was placed over a fulcrum with accusers at one end and the victim tied to a chair at the other. The chair was repeatedly dunked in water until the victim was proved guilty or innocent.

The first reference to dunking appeared in the 1754 BC Code of Hammurabi, stating that sorcerers were to be submerged in a stream and acquitted if they survived. Pliny the Elder, a Roman historian, also mentioned dunking as a punishment for witches in his *Naturalis Historia* of 70 AD. A 500 AD Saxon tome referred to a "scolding" stool and the *Domesday Book* of 1086 AD called the procedure Cathedra Stercoris.

In Medieval times, dunking was used to determine if one was a witch. Originally innocents floated, but this was later reversed so that only the innocent sank, the argument being that witches floated because they had renounced baptism in their deal with the Devil. Accidental drownings were common. A witch trial with dunking occurred in Hungary as late as 1728.

Ducking, or sometimes "cucking" stools, were also used as a punishment for scolds, disorderly women, dishonest tradesmen, women who bore illegitimate children, and prostitution. Unruly married couples were occasionally dunked back to back! Cucking comes from the Dutch "kakken" (not cuckold) meaning to defecate: because the chair used was often a chamber pot or commode. A Law against the common scold existed in New Jersey until 1972 when it was struck down as sex discrimination and violation of the 14th Amendment to the US Constitution.

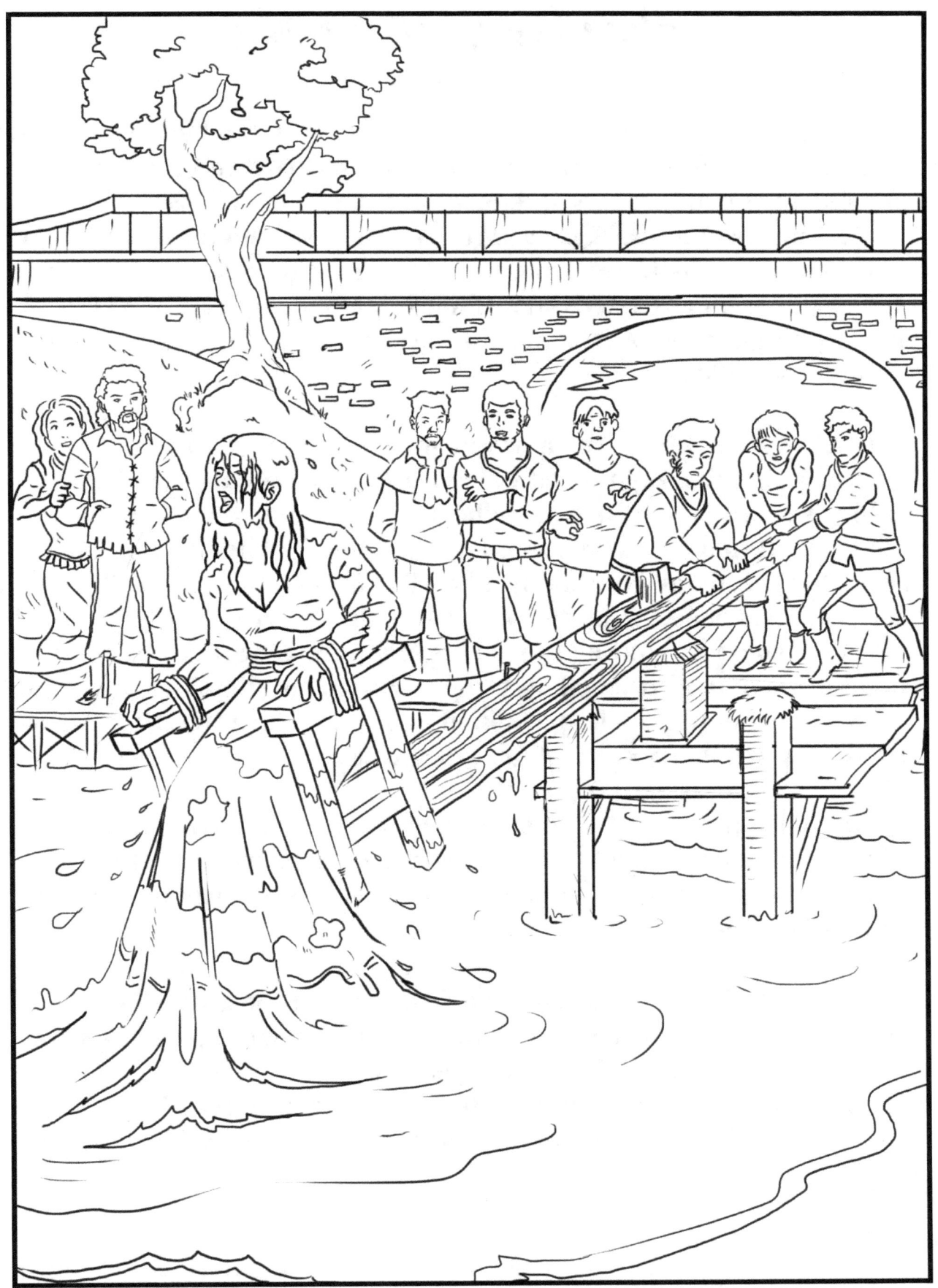

Shame Masks

Shame masks were a medieval European version of a badge of shame: a distinctive symbol or mark intended to humiliate and punish someone for an offence. Also known as "the Branks," "Scold's Bridle", or "Schandmaskes" as they were known in Germany, shame masks were a sadistic and cruel way to control offensive behaviors such as gossiping, hen pecking, nosiness, eavesdropping, or being greedy and gluttonous. The practice existed from the mid-1500s through the 1700s.

Typically made of iron, the mask or muzzle usually had exaggerated features indicating the type of behavior the victim had been accused of: big eyes or glasses for those who saw too much, giant ears for those who listened in on conversation, long tongues for gossips, and pig snouts for greedy or gluttonous acts. The mask would be padlocked to the offender's head for up to 24 hours as they were either led around town by a chain or confined to stocks in a public location. German masks often had a little bell on top to alert the public a shamed person was nearby. Some even had a spiked or sharp attachment that went into the mouth to prevent eating and speaking!

While occasionally used on men and children, their primary use was to intimidate and control "unruly" women, and to remind them of their place in the male-dominated social order of church-dominated Renaissance Europe.

The last recorded use of a scold's bridle was in 1856 at Bolton-le-Moors, Lancashire in the UK. Judging by the enormous number and variety of surviving masks in European collections, we can conclude this form of social control and torture was very popular. Especially ornate and well preserved shame masks sell at auction for thousands of dollars today!

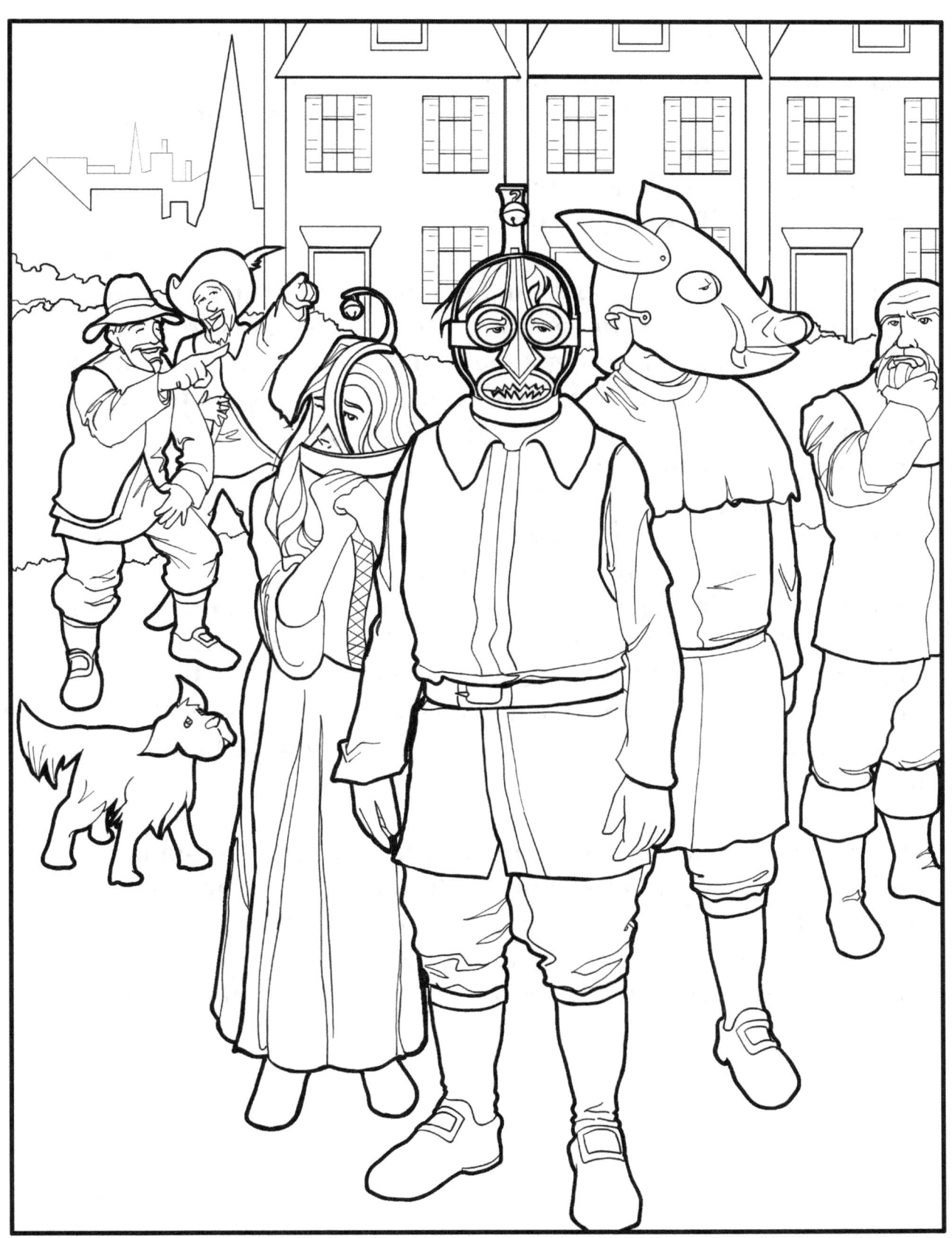

Chair of Torture

Today, we consider "seated torture" to be working eight hours a day in the bowels of a soulless air-conditioned corporate office, or enduring a two-hour commute home on choked freeways with only streaming audio and audio books for entertainment. In the old days, it was a slightly different proposition.

The Chair of Torture goes by many names: the Iron Chair, the Inquisition Chair, the Judas Chair, the Chinese Torture Chair. They all share the same terrifying appearance and construction though: spikes cover the back, arm-rests, seat, leg-rests and foot-rests. Some have straps and restraints that can be tightened to ensure the "guest" has a very tight and secure fit.

Typical usage consisted of a victim being tied to the chair, and the restraints progressively tightened until the desired confession was reached. Sometimes just watching another person get this treatment was enough to elicit a quick confession. For extra "spice," some inquisitors would add burning coals under the seat to flame broil the buttocks to a crisp. Torture could last a few minutes to a few days, the latter usually ending in a long agonizing death from blood loss and infection.

It is unclear when the Iron Chair was first developed and used (nobody seems to want to claim credit for some reason). Italy and Spain put the chairs away by the end of the 1700s. Germany removed them from use in the early 1800s, while Britain and several central European countries kept the chilling chairs in action right up to the end of the 1800s.

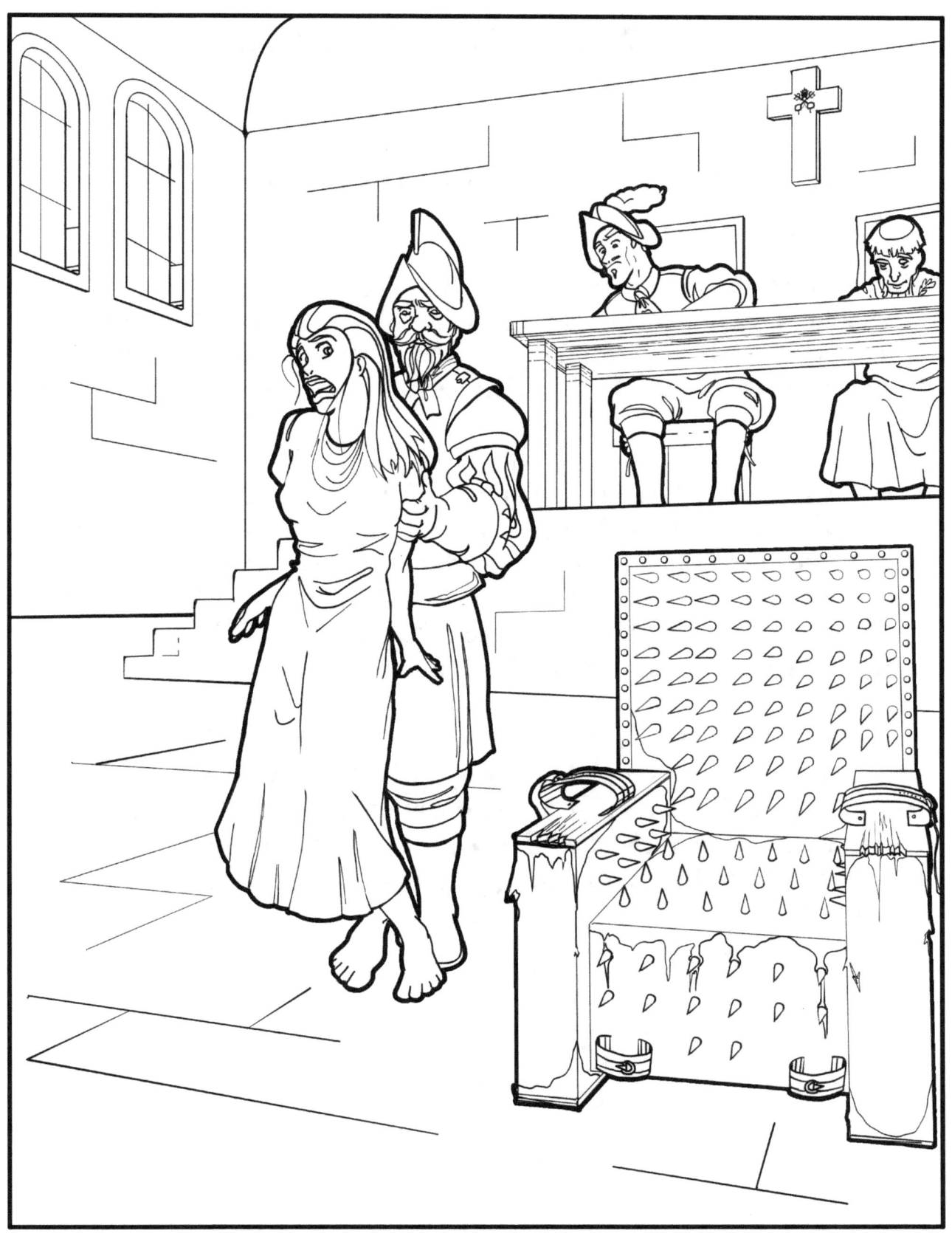

Wooden Horse

Guessing it's a lovingly handcrafted children's play thing?
Guess again…

The Wooden Horse, the Spanish donkey, Cavaletto Squarciapalle, the Chevalet… no matter what you call it, it still meant brutal torture. This horrible contraption got its name from the fact it resembled a horse: a large wooden board with a sharp V-wedge on top, held up by four legs.

Victims would be forced to "ride" the horse with legs spread on each side, with weights added to both feet until a confession was made. When additional incentive was needed, their feet could be held to a fire. If they refused to confess, additional weights were added until the rider's perineum ruptured, they lost buckets of blood, and their sacrum was finally broken with a loud, sickening snap.

Invented during- you guessed it- the Spanish Inquisition, these devices saw heavy use in colonial America. Sadly, the device was used during the American Civil War on Confederate prisoners. Union guards would make prisoners ride "the mule" for hours on end or until they passed out from blood loss and pain. Many were crippled for life, never able to walk again.

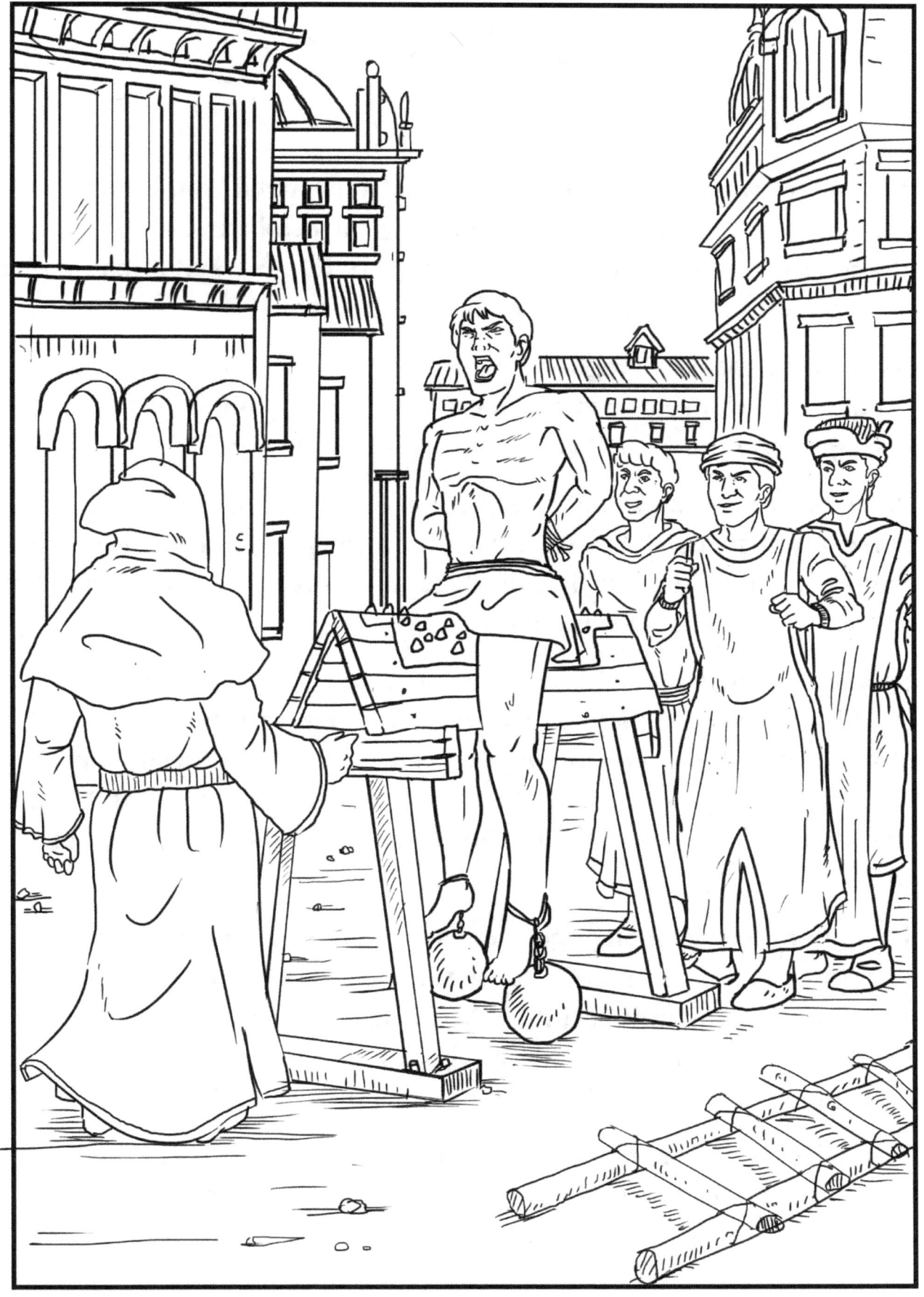

The Pillory

The pillory was a device made of a wooden or metal framework erected on a post, with holes for securing the head and hands, and was commonly used for punishment, public humiliation, and often further physical abuse. The pillory is related to the stocks.

Its use dates back to Anglo-Saxon times. The word stems from Old French Pellori, itself from medieval Latin Pilloria, of uncertain origin, perhaps a diminutive of Latin Pila "pillar, stone barrier."

Pillories were set up to hold people in marketplaces, crossroads, and other public places. They were used for a range of moral and political crimes, most notably for dishonest trading - the modern equivalent of implementing trading standards.

Spectators who watched the punishment, in addition to jeering and mocking the victim, often pelted the offender with rotten food, mud, offal, dead animals, and animal excrement. As a result, criminals were often very dirty by the end of their punishment, their faces and hair completely encrusted with the disgusting refuse they had been pelted with.

The pillory was formally abolished as a method of punishment in England and Wales in 1837, but the stocks remained in use (though extremely infrequently) until 1872. The last person to be pilloried in England was Peter James Bossy, who was convicted of "willful and corrupt perjury" in 1830.

Daniel Defoe was sentenced to the pillory in 1703 for Seditious libel. Regarded as a hero by the crowd, they pelted him with flowers.

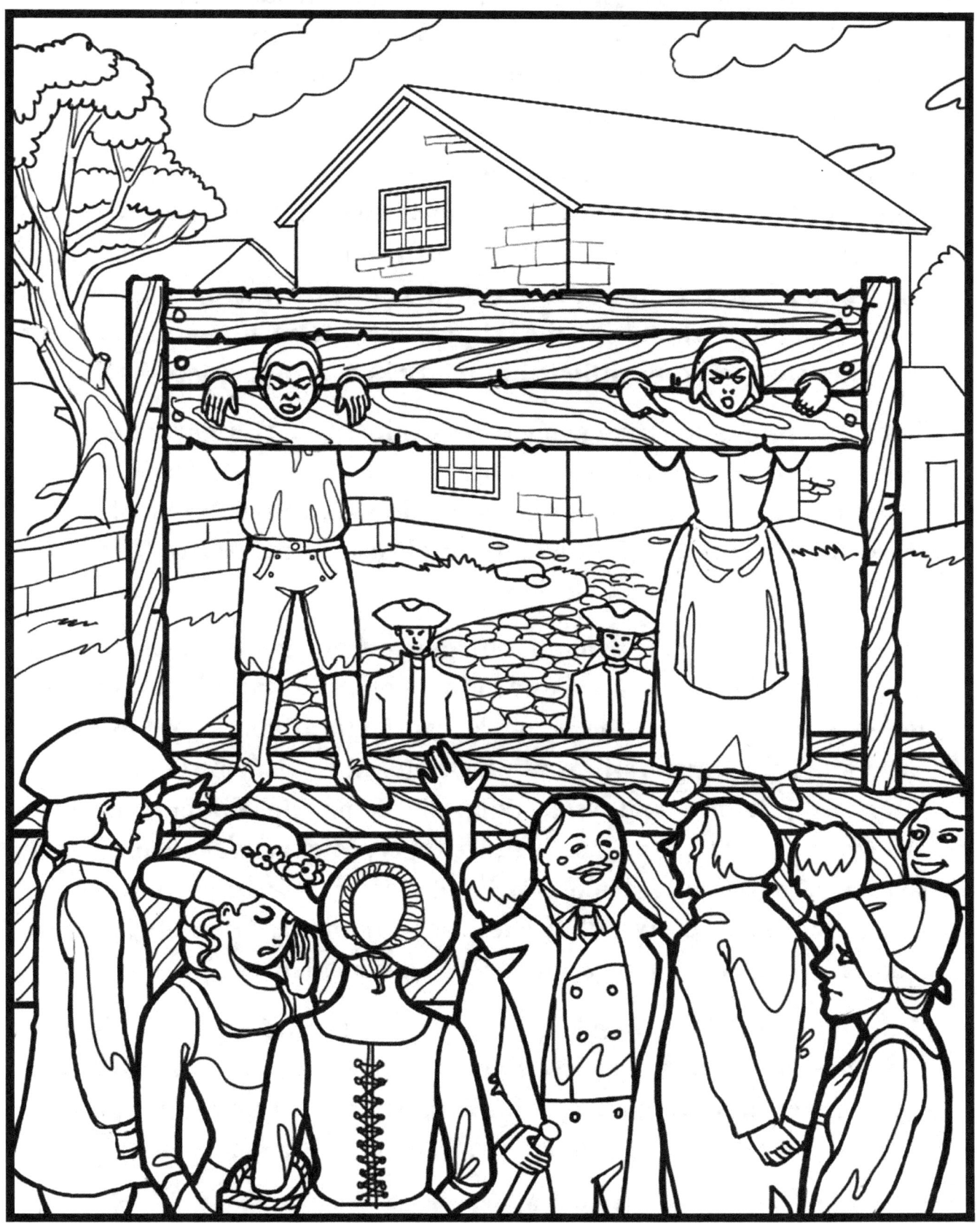

Flogging

Flogging, flagellation, whipping or lashing is the act of beating the human body with special implements such as whips, lashes, rods, switches, the cat o' nine tails, etc. The word comes from the Latin Flaggellum meaning "whip."

In ancient Sparta, young men were flogged as a test of their masculinity. Romans frequently flogged their victims prior to crucifixion and whipping was frequently used to discipline slaves in the United States. In the 18th and 19th centuries, European armies flogged soldiers who broke the military code. The maximum number of lashes that could be inflicted in the British Army reached 1,200!

Public whipping of (free) women ceased in 1817. Military flogging was abolished in the United States Army in 1861, the Royal Navy in 1879. Private whipping of men in prison continued in Britain until 1948. In the United States judicial flogging was last used in 1952 in Delaware when a wife beater got 20 lashes.

International law now prohibits flogging. The Universal Declaration on Human Rights and the Convention Against Torture prohibit torture and "cruel, inhuman, or degrading treatment or punishment." Sickeningly, caning is still routinely ordered by the courts in Singapore, Brunei, Malaysia, Indonesia, Tanzania, Zimbabwe and elsewhere. In 1994, an American teenager, Michael Fay, was sentenced to six cane strokes for vandalism in Singapore. In Iran, 30 college students received 99 lashes each for simply attending a "mixed gender" graduation party outside Tehran in 2016.

Did you know? The sound of a whip-crack is produced by a ripple in the material of the whip travelling towards the tip, rapidly escalating until it breaches the speed of sound, more than 30 times the speed of the initial movement in the handle. The crack is a small sonic boom!

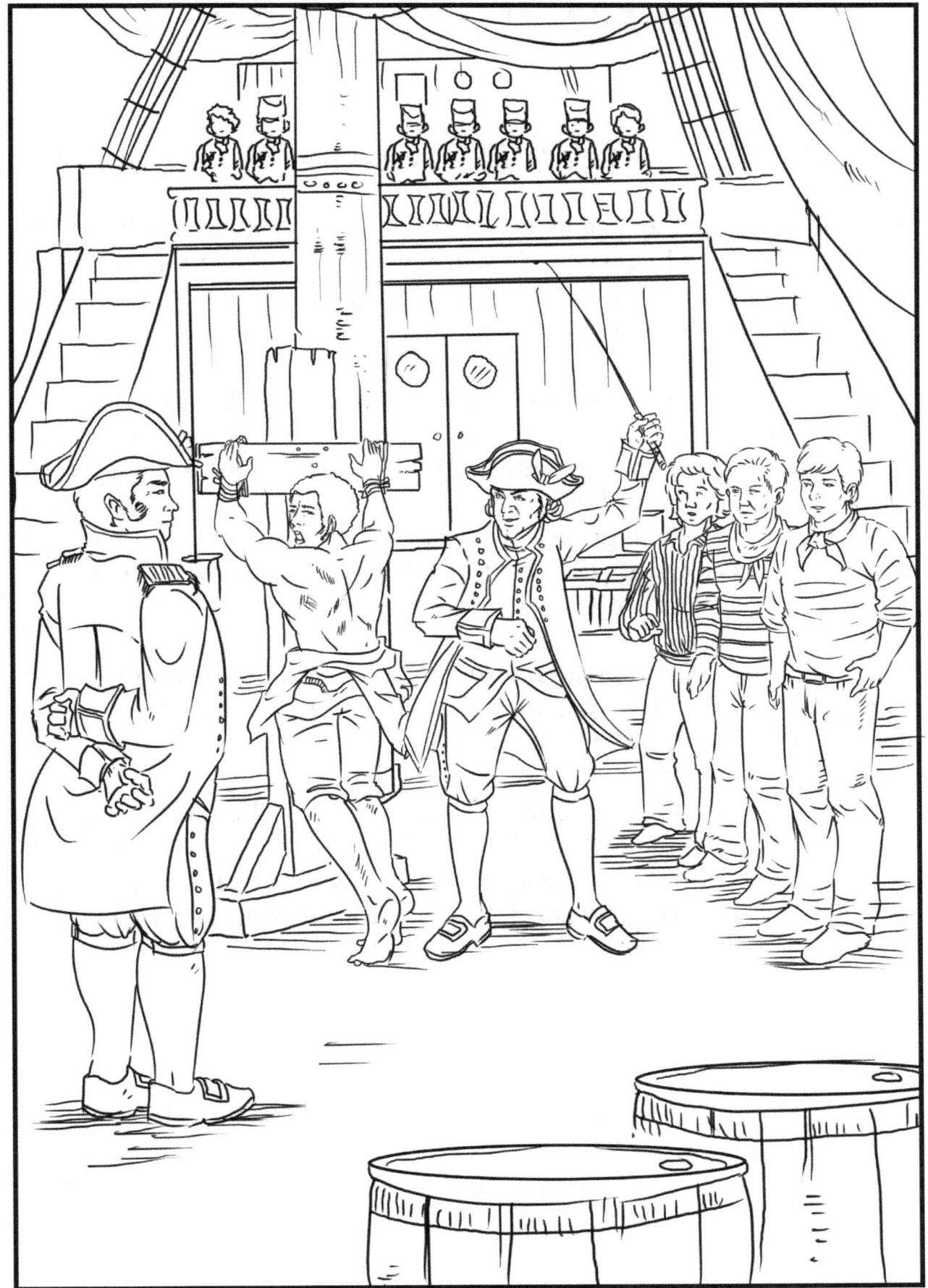

Spanish Tickler

The ability of this devilish device to cause laughter is questionable…

One could say the design of the Spanish Tickler is pretty cut and dry: several sharp steel claws are joined together to form a nightmarish hand. Also known by the deceptively cute name The Cat's Paw, a Spanish Tickler has four claws while a Cat's Paw has three.

The device was typically attached to a long pole and then dragged down the front and back sides of a tied up and defenseless victim. They often began with the limbs and slowly moved into the chest, back, neck and finally the face. The flesh would be shredded, with noses, ears, breasts, nipples, genitals, anything, torn off. This torture could often result in death. Most victims survived only by being subjected to short "laugh" sessions.

Used in most of Europe during the Middle Ages, this torture toy was very common in Spain, mostly during the Spanish Inquisition, which may explain the origin of the name.

A comedic "puppet" variation of this torture can be seen being performed on "Ludo" in Jim Henson's 1986 fantasy film *Labyrinth*, starring David Bowie and Jennifer Connelly. Instead of razor-sharp claws, the poor beast is being tortured with bitey lizard babies on sticks.

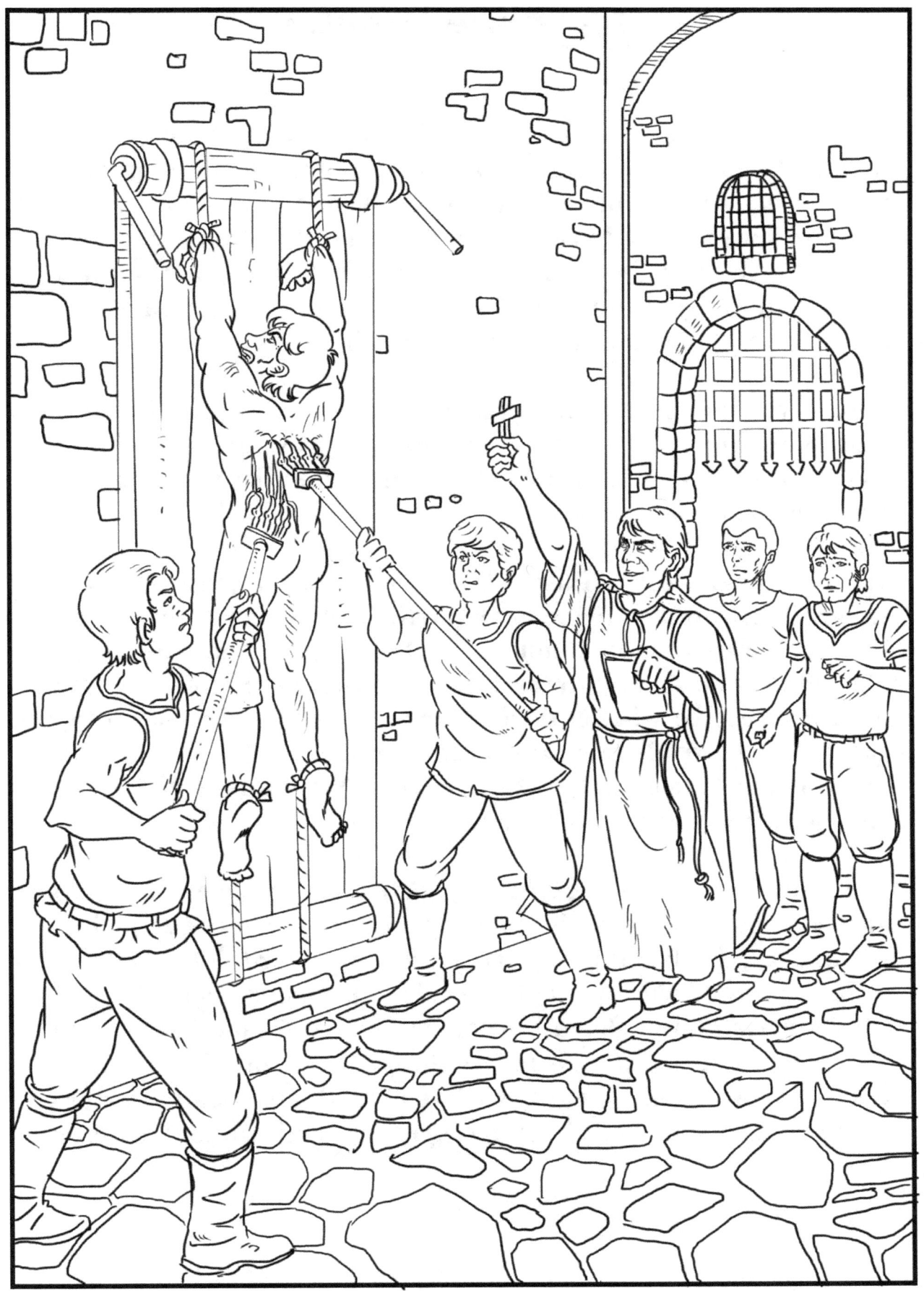

Strappado

Also known as The Corda, Strappado torture consists of tying a victim's hands behind their back, then tying a rope to their wrists, and hoisting them up off the ground by means of a pulley, beam or hook. This torture causes intense pain and often dislocates or even breaks the shoulders. Long term nerve and ligament damage or paralysis can result. Especially enthusiastic torturers can even add weights to the victim's feet to increase the stress and pain.

Probably in use since ancient times, this particular practice was made especially famous by – once again - the Spanish during the Inquisition. Images of the appalling practice appear in countless etchings and drawings from the period.

Niccolò Machiavelli, author of *The Prince*, was imprisoned by the Medici family and subjected to a particularly violent form of Strappado called Squassation where he was pulled up and down and allowed to drop several times. It is also believed to have been used to torture suspected witches during the Salem Witch Trials. Strappado was used extensively in Nazi concentration camps to punish rule breakers and was employed by the North Vietnamese on downed American pilots at the Hanoi Hilton.

One would think such a barbaric practice would have long ago been outlawed, but Strappado is still very popular in countries such as Libya, Iraq, Jordan and especially Turkey. After the failed 2016 coup in Turkey, hundreds of people were imprisoned in a sporting hall that was converted into a detention center a short distance from Ankara city center. The facility, owned by the Government of Turkey, was used to torture victims with a variety of methods, including mock executions, rape threats, beatings, spraying with ice cold water, and Strappado.

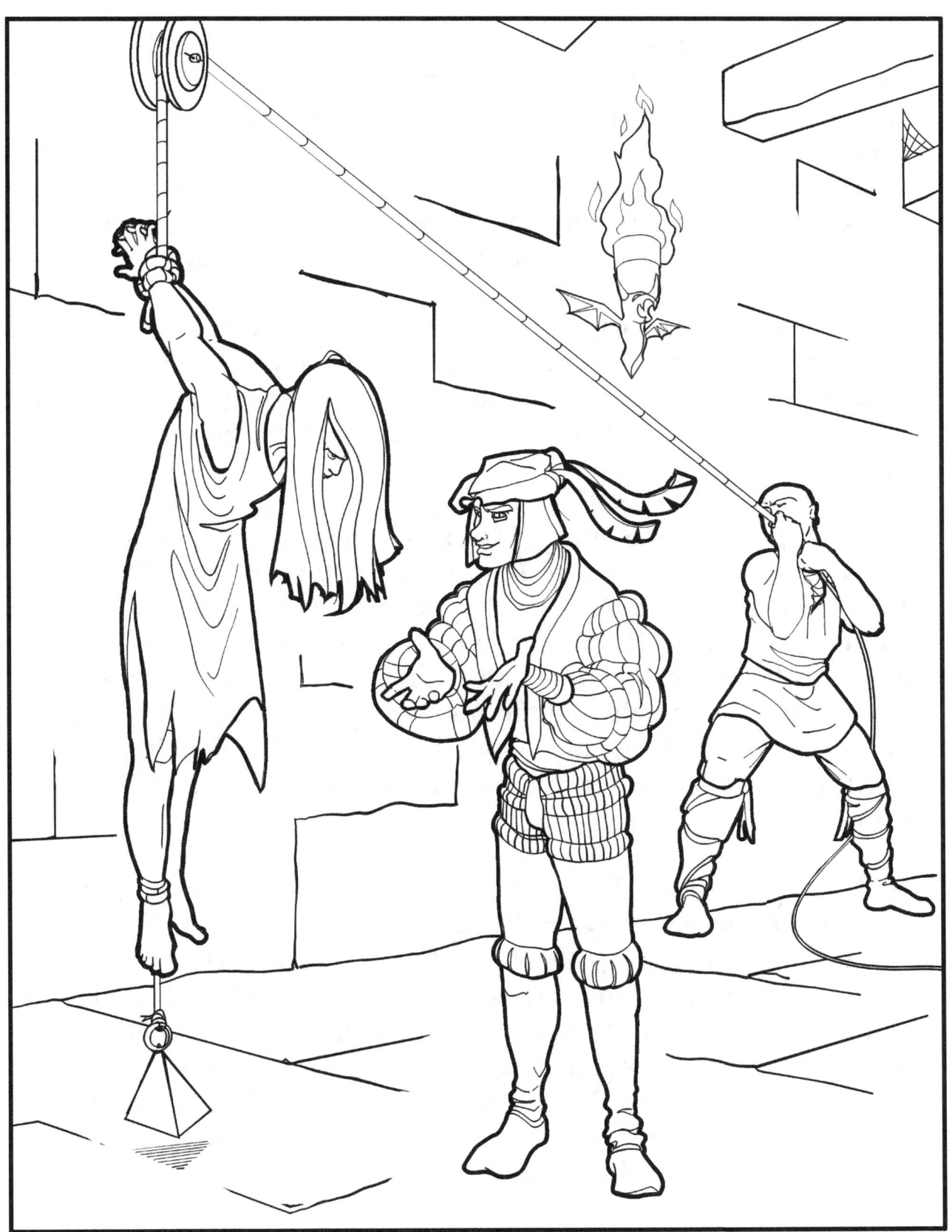

Waterboarding

Not to be confused with The Water Cure, waterboarding is a form of mock execution wherein the victim is bound and tied to a board, has their mouth and nose covered with a wet cloth, and then has water repeatedly poured over their face until they almost drown. Typically, the subject is tied to a board on their back at a slight incline with their head pointing down. When water does enter their nasal passages, their throat remains free of water, preventing accidental death.

Suffocation, unlike most tortures, leaves no marks on the body, which makes the crime easy to hide and deny. Waterboarding causes severe pain, lung and brain damage, long-lasting psychological damage, and often results in broken bones from involuntary spasms against restraints.

Waterboarding became the preferred way to extract confessions from prisoners during the Spanish Inquisition (what torture DIDN'T the Spanish use?). Its use has been documented by the Dutch East India Company in Indonesia, American troops during the Philippine–American War, the Japanese and Germans during WW2 on POWs, French paratroopers during the Algerian War, the Pinoche regime in Chile, the Khmer Rouge in Cambodia, the British Army in Northern Ireland, and - most famously - the CIA during the War or Terror following 911.

The U.S. Army Field Manual expressly prohibits soldiers from staging mock executions and they are illegal under international law. Khalid Sheikh Mohammed, responsible for the 911 attack, was waterboarded 183 times while being interrogated by the CIA in 2006. Vice President Dick Cheney denied waterboarding was torture and claimed it directly led the US to killing Osama Bin Laden. This claim was later disproven by the Senate Intelligence Committee which showed that the best intelligence used to find Bin Laden came from another prisoner through standard, noncoercive means.

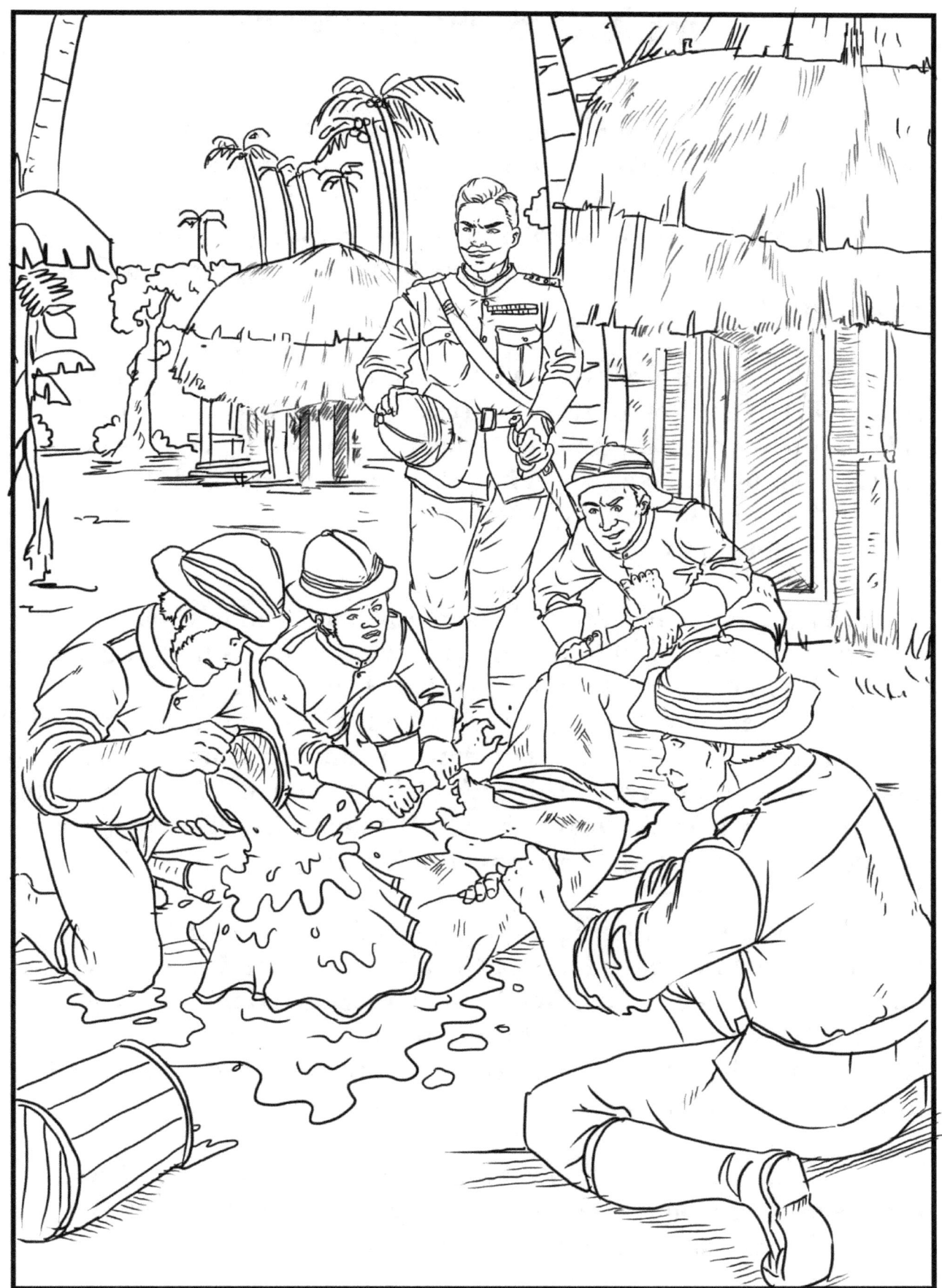

Foot Roasting

You know the expression, "hold their feet to the fire?" Well, this is where it comes from. In foot roasting, the victim was placed in stocks so their legs couldn't move. Red-hot coals were then placed under their feet. If they said what the interrogator wanted to hear, a shield was placed between their feet and the flames; if not, they had their feet roasted!

The practice was probably as ancient as fire itself. The Romans immobilized their prisoners and pressed red-hot iron plates to the soles of their feet. The Spanish Inquisition frequently employed a special technique: the accused had their feet secured and then basted with lard or oil, then slowly barbecued over a brazier of burning coals. Imagine the smell!

Foot roasting was one of the principal tortures used to extract supposed confessions of heresy and other accusations made against the Knights Templar after their arrest in October 1307. One Templar's feet were so savagely tortured that, as he was being carried back to his cell, various pieces of charred bone fell from his feet to the floor. A form of torture called "star kicking" supposedly began with Countess Elizabeth Bathory, who would place oiled bits of paper or string between the prisoner's toes and light the material on fire.

Cuauhtemoc, the last Aztec emperor, was famously foot-flambéd by the greedy conquistador Hernán Cortés. Furious at finding little gold and gems in Tenochtitlan after Cuauhtemoc's surrender, Cortés ordered the native noble's feet roasted until he revealed his secret treasure's hiding place. Cuauhtemoc revealed nothing. Cortés had him executed on false charges shortly afterwards.

Allegedly, the Russian Federal Security Service (modern KGB) continues to use foot-roasting to this day, using flat, hot clothes irons held to the soles of a victim's feet to loosen their tongue.

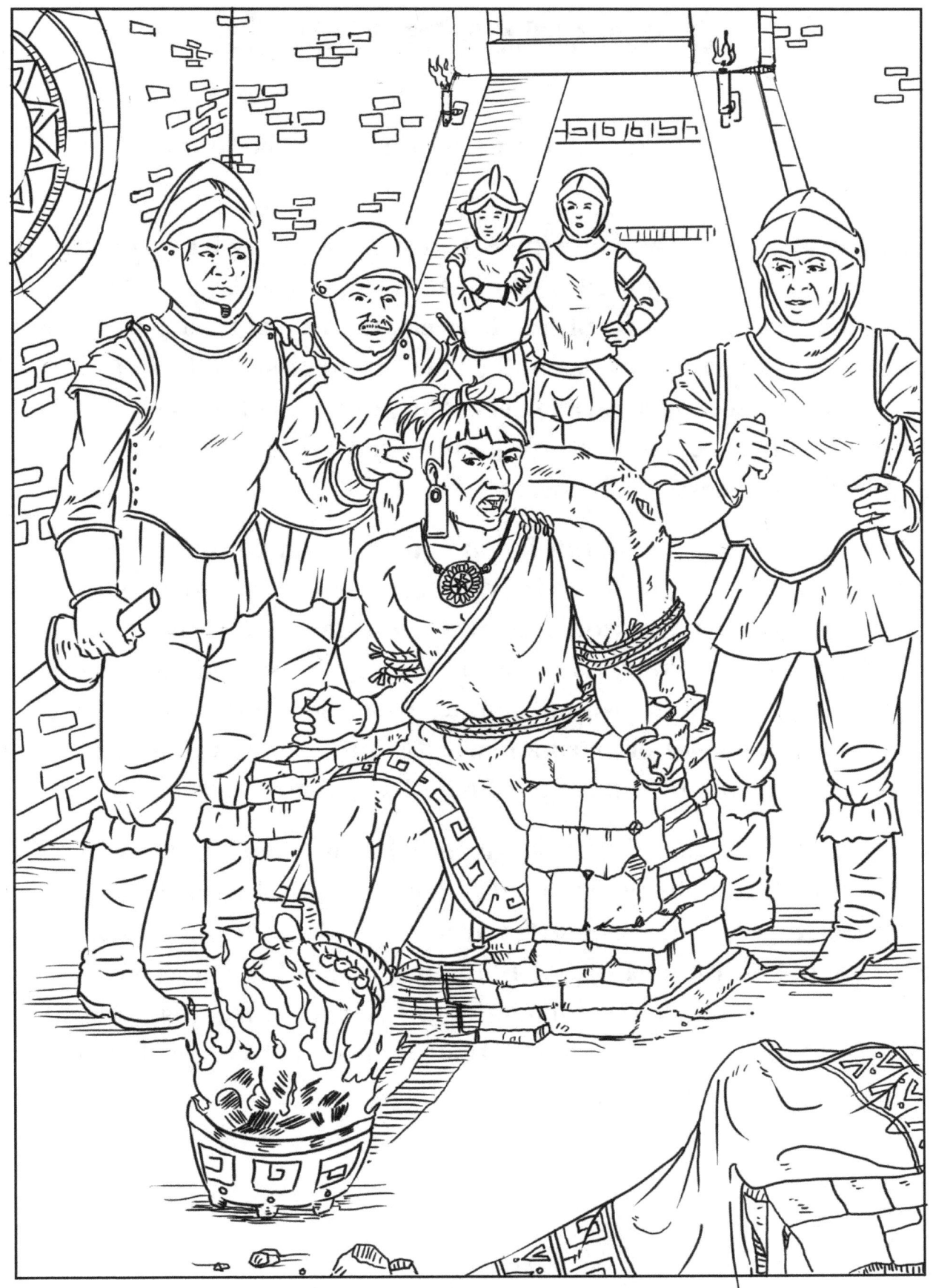

Heretic's Fork

Things were not looking up for prisoners subjected to this nasty device…

The Heretic's Fork was a torture device, loosely consisting of a length of metal with two opposed bi-pronged forks as well as an attached belt or strap. The device was placed between the breast bone and throat just under the chin, with a small collar supporting the fork, forcing the victim to hold their head erect. The punishment made it nearly impossible to talk. The victim's hands were tied behind their back to prevent any chance of escape.

A person wearing it couldn't fall asleep: the moment their head dropped with fatigue, the prongs pierced their throat or chest, causing great pain. The victim would be awake for days, which made confessions more likely. Even swallowing one's own saliva was torture as the strap bound the Adam's apple, creating suffocation. This naughty necklace often permanently disfigured the neck of the victim, as well as causing infections and sometimes death.

Usually the Heretic's Fork was given to blasphemers, liars, or people who spoke the lord's name in vain. Popular with the - wait for it - Spanish Inquisition, these little horrors had the following phrase engraved, Abiuro, meaning "I renounce, recant". Even persistent heretics of the Church would confess when they wore this accessory for a long time. Many times, this torture was used as a prelude to being burned at the stake.

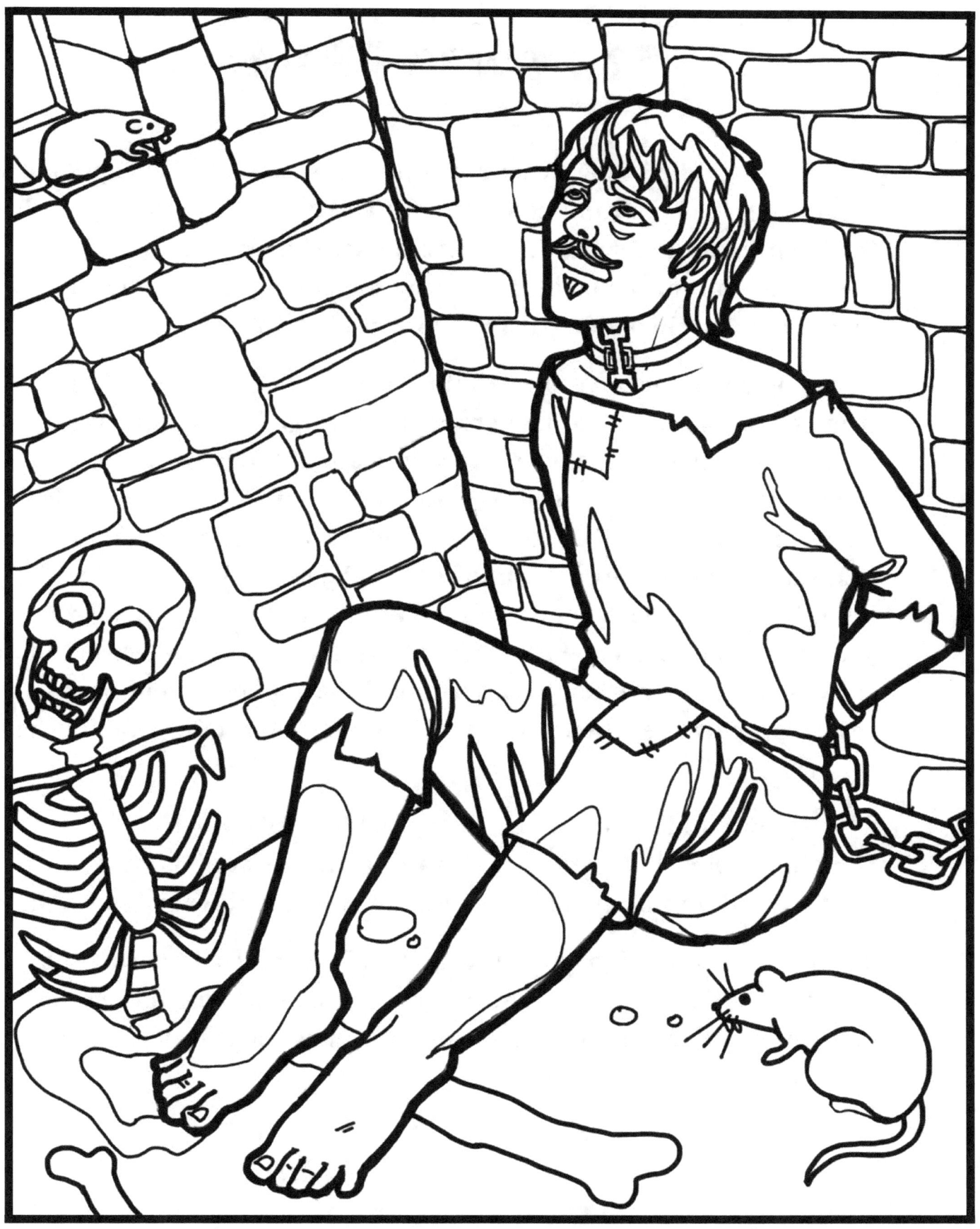

Shrew's Fiddle

A Shrew's Fiddle or neck violin was a variation of the yoke, pillory or rigid irons. The restraint consisted of three holes: one was a large hole for the neck and the other two were smaller holes for the wrists, locked in front of the face. In this way the person could be easily directed and pulled along a street for public humiliation.

It was originally used in the Middle Ages as a way of punishing women who were caught bickering or fighting. This female frustrator was very popular in medieval Germany and Austria, where it was known as a Halsgeige, meaning "neck viola" or "neck violin." Bells were sometimes attached to this portable pillory to let villagers know that the victim was approaching so that she might be mocked and humiliated. Another version was a "double fiddle" by which two people could be attached together face-to-face, forcing them to talk to each other. They were not released until the argument had been resolved - perhaps a better form of marriage counseling than we have today!

The Shrew's Fiddle was in use until the late 1800s when Enlightenment ideas superseded traditional Christian morality. Torture and humiliation slowly became eradicated from Christendom.

Today modern versions of the shrew's fiddle are used for restraint and humiliation by BDSM enthusiasts. Although some devices are made of hand-carved wood and resemble a violin, stainless steel is now the preferred manacle material.

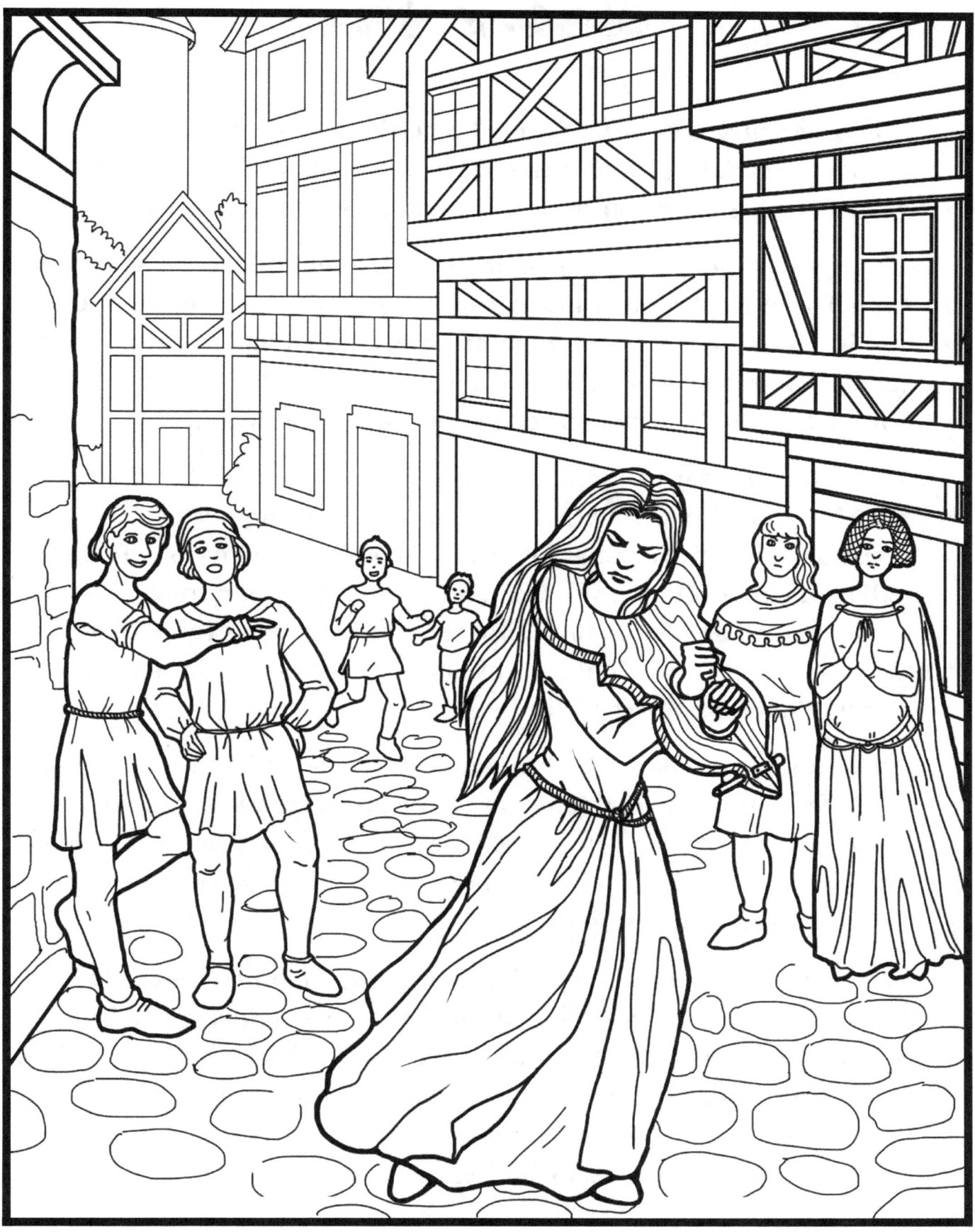

Water Cure

The water cure is a form of forced ingestion in which the victim is forced to drink large quantities of water in a short time. It results in gastric distension, water intoxication and – sometimes - death.

The victim would be tied up and have their mouth forced open with a funnel or other device. If the prisoner didn't drink the liquid, they would drown. Their stomach painfully expanded and to top things off, they would sometimes be punched or stomped on the belly until they vomited. Then the whole process would start over again.

Water torture was used extensively in France from the Middle Ages to the 17th and 18th centuries. It was known as "being put to the question," with the ordinary question involving the forcing of one gallon of water into the stomach and the extraordinary question involving two gallons. A form of water cure known as the Swedish drink was used by various international troops in the German states during the Thirty Years' War.

American troops used it on Filipinos during the Philippine–American War. The Japanese used it against British, American and Chinese soldiers during WW2. Human Rights Watch reports that in the 2000s, security forces in Uganda sometimes forced a detainee to lie face up under an open water spigot.

Water intoxication can result from drinking too much water. This has resulted in several deaths in fraternities in the US during "Hell Week." Matthew Carrington was hazed to death by Chi Tau of Chico State (California) in 2005 via the forcing of pushups and the drinking of water from a five gallon bottle. His killers only received sentences ranging from ninety days to one year in jail.

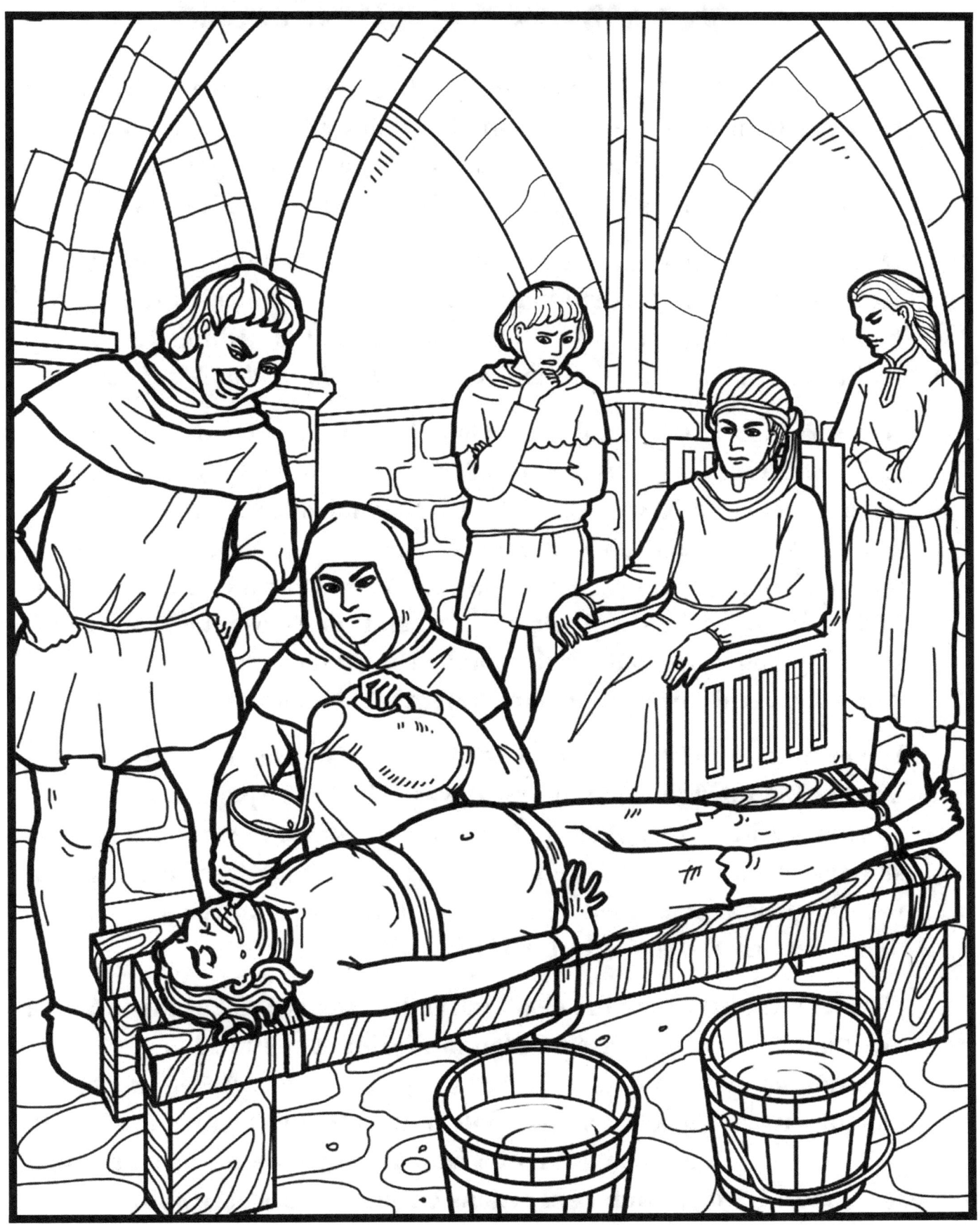

Drunkard's Cloak

The Drunkard's Cloak was actually a barrel with a hole in the top for the head to pass through. Two smaller holes were made in the sides for the arms. Victims were clothed in this device and paraded about town for public humiliation and punishment for intoxication.

Drunkenness was first made a civil offence in England by the Ale Houses Act 1551. The drunkard's cloak, sometimes called the Newcastle Cloak, became a common method of punishing the inebriated during the Commonwealth of England (1649–1660).

A description of the drunkard's cloak appeared in Ralph Gardiner's *England's Grievance Discovered* of 1655. A John Willis claimed to have travelled to Newcastle and seen, "men drove up and down the streets, with a great tub, or barrel, opened in the sides, with a hole in one end, to put through their heads, and to cover their shoulders and bodies, down to the small of their legs, and then close the same, called the new fashioned cloak, and so make them march to the view of all beholders; and this is their punishment for drunkards, or the like."

It was used in Delft Holland in 1634 and at The Hague in 1660. It was used in Denmark in 1784, where it was called the Spanish Mantle. In Germany, they called it the Schandmantel, which means "coat of shame." A liquor thief during the American Civil War was punished with the cloak, placarded with "I am a thief," and marched with a drum beating the rogue's march through the streets.

The last known use of the cloak in the US was in 1932 at the infamous "hellhole" Sunbeam Prison Camp in Florida. On June 2, a petty criminal named Maillefert refused to work. He was placed in a barrel, naked, with his head through a hole in the top and thrown in a sweat box. He chewed his way out and escaped, only to be captured a short time later. He died under suspicious circumstances only hours later. So much for "The Sunshine State"…

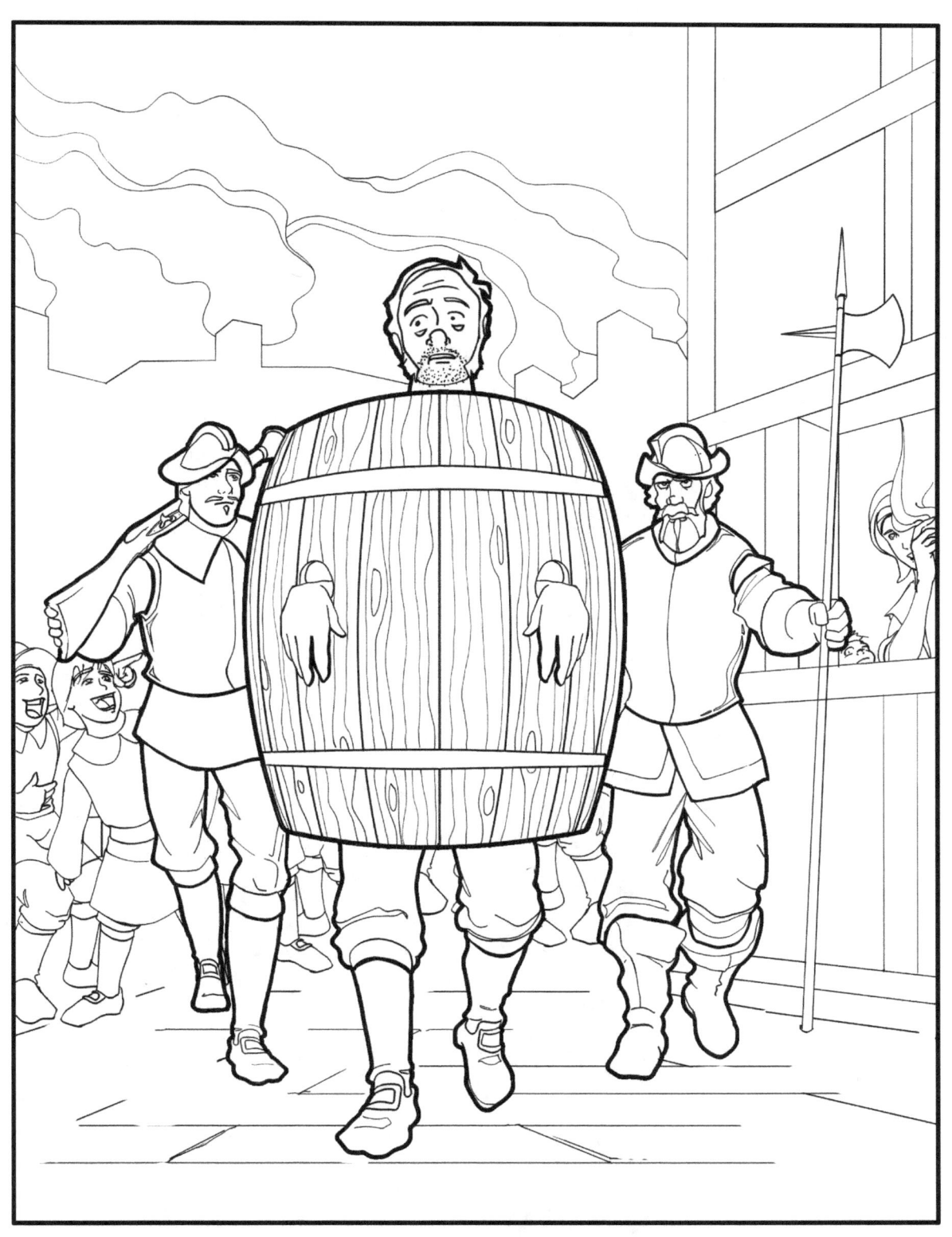

Attributions

Color Test Page

Skull icon designed by **Eucalyp** from www.flaticon.com

Knife icon designed by **Madebyoliver** from www.flaticon.com

Hammer icon designed by **Madebyoliver** from www.flaticon.com

Broken heart icon designed by **Madebyoliver** from www.flaticon.com

Blood drop icon designed by **Kirill Kazachek** from www.flaticon.com

Illustrations:

The following freelance illustrators worked on the following plates:

Mudjib Pradana: https://www.freelancer.com/u/mudjib

The Rack, Waterboarding. Foot Roasting, Flogging, The Wooden Horse, The Spanish Tickler, Dunking, Thumbscrews.

Joe Cassada: https://www.freelancer.com/u/JoeCassada

Keelhauling, Drunkard's Coat, Strappado, Chair of Torture, Mask of Shame, Iron Maiden.

Alina N: https://www.freelancer.com/u/LTailor

The Water Cure, Shrew's Fiddle, Heretic's Fork, The Pillory.

All illustrations property of Verbania Toys & Games

Copyright © 2017

All Rights Reserved